A Thanksgiving Tale of Friendship and Gratitude

The Forest's Thanksgiving Feast

WRITTEN BY
J.P. ANTHONY WILLIAMS

Thank You - Your <u>Free</u> Gift

Thank you for your interest in "A Thanksgiving Tale of Friendship and Gratitude" You can download your exclusive <u>FREE</u> copy of this amazing Activity Book by scanning the QR code with your phone camera. And don't forget to check out the other Free coloring book at the end of the book.

Once upon a time in the heart of the vibrant forest, a bustling community of animals went about their daily lives. There was Rosie the rabbit, Benny the bear, Sammy the squirrel, Bella the bee, Chip the chipmunk, and Ollie the owl, among others.

One sunny morning, as the animals gathered to chat beneath the towering oak tree, they realized that Thanksgiving was approaching and they wanted to celebrate it. But they also needed to start their harvest so they could store enough food for the long, chilly winter months ahead.

"I've planted the most delicious carrots this year, the juiciest in the whole forest!" Rosie, the nimble rabbit, proudly exclaimed.

"And I've been gathering leaves and mushrooms, perfect for a Thanksgiving feast!" Chip, the chipmunk, chimed in.

"We have been busy all summer making the sweetest honey ever!" Bella and her fellow bees buzzed with excitement.

Benny the bear, had been watching over some wild berry plants, ensuring they thrived for the harvest. "And I've been storing up these wild berries for this special day," he added.

But as the forest animals began to make plans for a grand Thanksgiving feast, ominous clouds rolled in, and a distant rumble of thunder echoed through the trees. "Oh no! A storm is brewing!" cried Ollie the owl, his large eyes wide with concern.

And so, the forest animals leaped into action. Rosie began digging up her plump carrots with the help of Benny.
"Careful, Benny! Those carrots are the pride of the forest," chuckled Rosie, passing her carrots to Benny, who carefully brushed off the dirt.

Sammy, known for his tree-climbing skills, was on a mission to gather acorns from the tallest oaks. "I've got the best acorns in the whole forest!" he declared proudly. Ollie the owl assisted by guiding him to the ripest treasures hidden among the branches.

Meanwhile, Bella and her fellow bees worked tirelessly, collecting honeycombs and storing them safely in the hollow of a tree. Bella buzzed around joyfully, saying, "Our sweet honey will make this Thanksgiving extra special!"

As the forest animals worked in harmony, the wind began to pick up, making it challenging for Chip to gather mushrooms without the wind blowing them away. Benny the bear, with his strong paws, lent a helping hand. "Hold tight, Chip! We'll make sure those mushrooms don't escape!" he chuckled.

Then it was Rosie's turn to help Benny collect the wild berries. Their teamwork made berry picking a breeze as they gently reached for the juiciest berries in the thickest brambles.

With teamwork, the animals managed to gather all their harvest in the nick of time. As the first raindrops splashed down, they huddled beneath a broad mushroom cap to stay dry.

As the rain stopped, the animals gathered under the old oak tree to share their harvest, creating a lavish Thanksgiving feast.

They passed around delicious dishes made from their own harvest – carrot soup, honey-drizzled acorn squash, nut-stuffed mushrooms, and a colorful salad of leaves and berries.

As they feasted, they couldn't help but smile at what they had accomplished together. Benny raised a paw and said, "I'm thankful for all of you, my friends. Together, we make a great team."

"Yes. With friendship and a dash of determination, we can overcome any challenge. Here's to the best Thanksgiving ever!" Sammy chimed in.

With a heartwarming smile, Rosie raised a carrot in her paw and said, "And I'm thankful for the bountiful forest that provides us with food and shelter, and for all of you, my dear friends, who make each day an adventure worth sharing. Happy Thanksgiving!"

And so, beneath the shelter of the mighty oak tree, the animal friends learned the true meaning of Thanksgiving – gratitude for one another and the beauty of sharing with one another.

Wishing you a blessed Thanksgiving filled with Peace and Love.

THE END

Scan QR code to check out the other books in this series

Thank You - Your <u>Free</u> Gift

Thank you for reading "A Thanksgiving Tale of Friendship and Gratitude".

I hope you enjoyed it and if you have a minute to spare, I would be extremely grateful if you could post <u>a short review on my book's Amazon page</u>

To show my gratitude, I am offering a FREE copy of this amazing <u>Animals Coloring Book.</u> Download your free copy by scanning the QR code with your phone

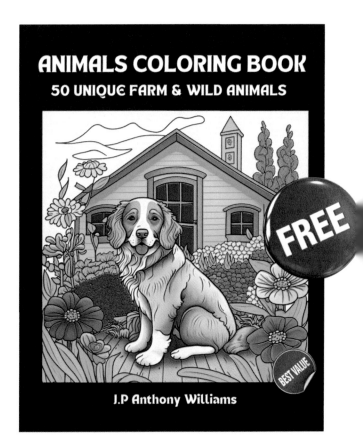

What's Next

Scan QR Code for other Books in this Series

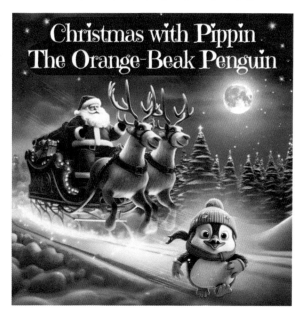

What's Next
Scan QR Code for other Books in this Series

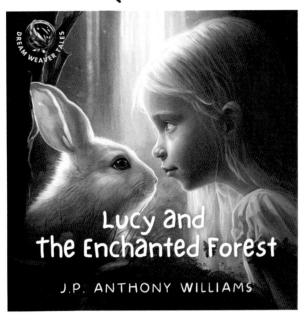

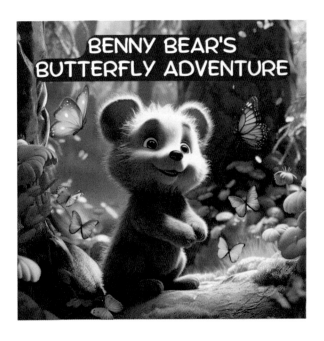

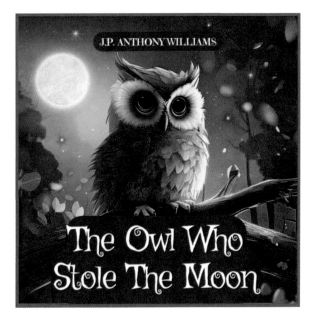

What's Next
Scan QR Code for other Books in this Series

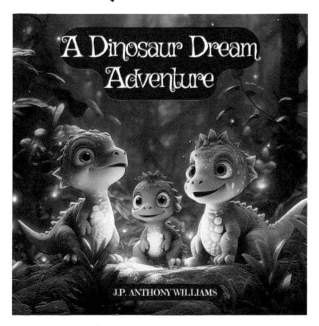

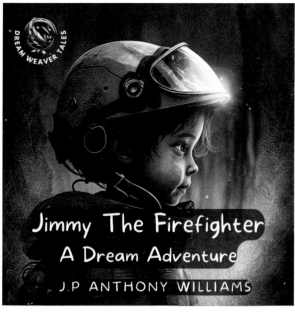

About the Author

J.P Anthony Williams is a bestselling children's book author, known for his enchanting tales and vivid illustrations. His stories are loved by young readers all over the world.

Born and raised in a small town, J.P developed a love of nature and storytelling at an early age. He spent his childhood exploring the woods and fields near his home, and he loved nothing more than curling up with a good book.

J.P's stories are known for their vivid imagery and richly-detailed illustrations. He takes inspiration from the natural world and from the myths and legends of his childhood, and he weaves them into tales that are both entertaining and educational.

In his free time, J.P can be found exploring new places and seeking inspiration for his next book. He is also a big advocate for environmental conservation, and often uses his platform to raise awareness about nature and its preservation.

Special thanks to my wife and kids for their endless support.